Let's Fly
DRONES

by Wendy Hinote Lanier

FOCUS
READERS

www.focusreaders.com

Focus Readers is distributed by North Star Editions:
sales@northstareditions.com | 888-417-0195

Produced for Focus Readers by Red Line Editorial.

Photographs ©: Dmitry Kalinovsky/Shutterstock Images, cover, 1; BravoKiloVideo/ Shutterstock Images, 4–5; byvalet/Shutterstock Images, 7; hedgehog111/Shutterstock Images, 8–9; ©Imperial War Museum (H 10307), 11; Nor Gal/Shutterstock Images, 12; Carla Thomas/AFRC/NASA, 14–15; Jacob Lund/Shutterstock Images, 17; Stock image/ Shutterstock Images, 19, 29; Shi Yali/Shutterstock Images, 20–21; bymandesigns/ Shutterstock Images, 22–23; ImagineChina/AP Images, 25; goodluz/Shutterstock Images, 27

Library of Congress Cataloging-in-Publication Data
Library of Congress Cataloging-in-Publication Data is available on the Library of Congress website.

ISBN
978-1-64185-336-1 (hardcover)
978-1-64185-394-1 (paperback)
978-1-64185-510-5 (ebook pdf)
978-1-64185-452-8 (hosted ebook)

Printed in the United States of America
Mankato, MN
October, 2018

About the Author

Wendy Hinote Lanier is a native Texan and former elementary teacher who writes and speaks for children and adults on a variety of topics. She is the author of more than 30 books for children and young adults.

TABLE OF CONTENTS

CHAPTER 1

A BIG DAY FOR DRONES

A buzzing sound fills the air. Xponential has begun. People come from all over to attend this event. They crowd into a huge hall. Inside, companies show what their drones can do.

 A drone flies at a trade show in Las Vegas.

The drones are many shapes and sizes. Some are as big as airplanes. Others can fit in a person's hand.

Experts give talks. They explain new ways drones can be used. There are contests, too. Teams work to build drones. They have

FUN FACT

Xponential is a trade show for **unmanned** vehicles. More than 600 companies bring their drones and robots to show off how they work.

A racing drone speeds past the finish line.

32 hours to finish. The best drones win prizes.

Visitors can even watch drone races. Pilots steer the drones along a course. They zoom toward the finish line.

CHAPTER 2

EARLY IDEAS

Nikola Tesla invented the first drone in the late 1800s. He used radio waves to control a toy boat. Viewers were fascinated. So were **military** leaders. They thought drones could be used in war.

 Drones are controlled by remotes that use radio waves.

In the 1910s, the US Army tried using drones. The drones were called unmanned **aerial** vehicles (UAVs). UAVs looked similar to airplanes. But they did not have

WHAT'S IN A NAME?

Early UAVs were used for target practice. The British used a kind of UAV called the Queen Bee. Gunners tried to shoot it down as it flew through the air. The UAV made a buzzing noise. The noise seemed to drone on and on. For this reason, UAVs became known as drones.

 The British army used Queen Bee UAVs during World War II (1939–1945).

pilots. Instead, people used radio signals to control them.

The United States tried making drones that could drop bombs. A system guided the drones to their targets. But this system was hard to make. Several tests failed.

 Transistors are used in many products that send and receive radio signals.

Still, inventors kept working. By the 1940s, UAVs could collect information. They could be used as weapons, too.

In the 1960s, **transistors** became smaller. As a result, they could be used to make smaller drones. They cost less, too. More people could buy drones.

In the late 1900s, drones began using **digital** controls. The controls allowed drones to do more complex tasks. They also made drones less expensive. People could own and use drones as a hobby.

FUN FACT

Not all drones can fly. Some move along the ground. Others go through the water.

CHAPTER 3

DRONE DESIGNS

Drones can have several designs. Fixed-wing drones look similar to airplanes. Other drones look like helicopters. Many drones have several **rotors**. These drones are called rotary drones.

 NASA tests a fixed-wing drone.

A quadcopter is one kind of rotary drone. It has a light frame and four rotors. A quadcopter also has a computer and a power source.

Most drones get power from a battery. This battery is not heavy. It can be recharged. The battery

FUN FACT

Quadcopters are the most common kind of drone. They are also the easiest to fly. Their rotors keep them steady.

 A woman uses a smartphone to control a drone.

powers the drone's motors. A motor
makes each rotor's blade spin.

Each drone has a **transmitter**.
This part helps people control the
drone. It sends signals to the drone.

17

A receiver on the drone picks up the signals. It sends the information to the drone's computer. The computer controls the drone's movement.

Some drones use joysticks as transmitters. Other drones are

IN THE AIR

A quadcopter's computer uses sensors to keep the drone steady. It also sends signals to the motors. The motors control the rotors. Motors make the blades spin faster or slower. By changing the rotors' speed, a person can move the drone through the air.

PARTS OF A DRONE

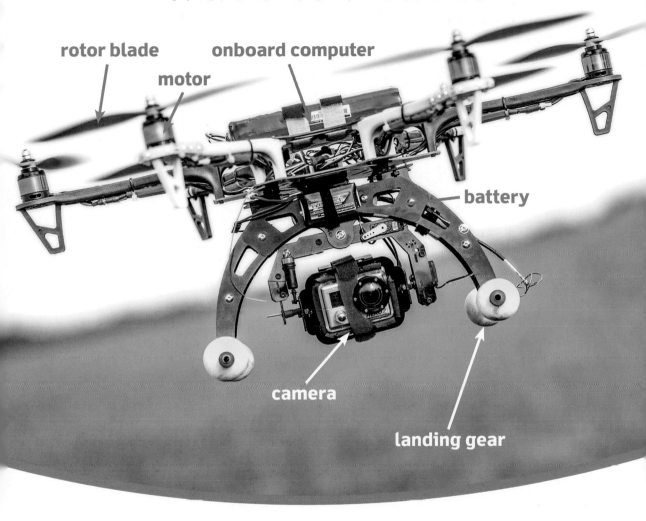

rotor blade

onboard computer

motor

battery

camera

landing gear

controlled using **apps**. The app is
usually on a phone or tablet. People
use these devices to fly the drone.

STEERING ITSELF

An onboard computer allows a drone to do some tasks on its own. For example, some drones can fly back to their starting point. To do so, they use a **GPS** chip. The chip tells the drone where it is. It also remembers the drone's takeoff spot.

Drones can fly to a certain spot and hover. A drone uses its GPS chip to find the spot. Another instrument in the drone measures the height. It makes sure the drone stays in the same place. The GPS chip helps hold it there, even in high winds.

A hexacopter, a drone with six rotors, records video as it flies.

CHAPTER 4

DRONES TODAY

Drones are easier to fly and own than ever before. In the United States, some cost as little as $25. Other drones are more advanced. These drones cost more. But they can do more tasks.

 Many drones use cameras to record video from the air.

For example, many drones have cameras and sensors. These parts help the drone land slowly. That way, the drone is less likely to crash. A drone might also use its cameras

RULES FOR FLIGHT

Most countries have rules for flying drones. For example, in the United States, drones cannot fly more than 400 feet (122 m) above the ground. And people must get permission to fly drones within 5 miles (8.0 km) of any airport. These rules help make sure a drone will not hit an airplane and cause a crash.

 A drone delivers a package in China.

to create a map. The map helps the

drone move safely around objects.

Some drones can take pictures or

videos. The drones help with many

jobs. Some drones monitor traffic.

They show what roads look like from above. Some drones help people study the weather. Drones are also used to deliver packages.

New drones are being invented all the time. As more businesses use drones, more people are needed to fly them. In fact, some people train

FUN FACT

Drones are used to film some movies. They fly above the actors and record video from the air.

 Engineers work to invent new kinds of drones.

to be **professional** drone pilots. But many other people fly drones just for fun.

FOCUS ON
DRONES

Write your answers on a separate piece of paper.

1. Write a paragraph that describes some of the ways drones are used today.

2. Which type of drone would you most like to own? Why?

3. Which type of drone has wings like an airplane?
   A. quadcopter
   B. fixed-wing drone
   C. rotary drone

4. How could a drone help people study the weather?
   A. A drone could fly up into the air and take pictures of a storm.
   B. A drone could carry scientists up inside a cloud.
   C. A drone could use its rotors to stop rain from falling.

5. What does **monitor** mean in this book?

*Some drones **monitor** traffic. They show what roads look like from above.*

    A. change

    B. stop

    C. watch

6. What does **advanced** mean in this book?

*Other drones are more **advanced**. These drones cost more. But they can do more tasks.*

    A. having more parts or features

    B. having fewer parts or features

    C. able to do fewer tasks

Answer key on page 32.

GLOSSARY

aerial
Taking place in the air.

apps
Computer programs that complete a task.

digital
Having to do with information used on a computer.

GPS
A navigation system that uses satellites to figure out location.

military
Having to do with soldiers or armed forces.

professional
Paid to do something as a job, rather than doing it just for fun.

rotors
Horizontal sets of spinning blades that provide lift.

transistors
Devices that control the flow of electricity.

transmitter
A device that sends out radio waves or other signals.

unmanned
Without a person or pilot inside.

TO LEARN MORE

BOOKS

Clasky, Leonard. *We Build a Drone*. New York: Rosen Publishing, 2018.

Hustad, Douglas. *Discover Drones*. Minneapolis: Lerner Publications, 2017.

Marsico, Katie. *Drones*. New York: Scholastic, 2016.

Scott, Mairghread. *Robots and Drones: Past, Present, and Future*. New York: First Second, 2018.

NOTE TO EDUCATORS

Visit **www.focusreaders.com** to find lesson plans, activities, links, and other resources related to this title.

INDEX

B
battery, 16, 19

C
cameras, 19, 24
computer, 16, 18–19, 20

F
fixed-wing drones, 15

G
GPS chip, 20

M
motors, 17–19

P
pilots, 7, 11, 27

Q
quadcopters, 16, 18
Queen Bee, 10

R
races, 7
receiver, 18
rotary drones, 15–16
rotors, 15–18

S
sensors, 18, 24

T
Tesla, Nikola, 9
transistors, 12
transmitter, 17–19

U
unmanned aerial vehicles (UAVs), 10
US Army, 10–11

V
video, 25–26

Answer Key: 1. Answers will vary; **2.** Answers will vary; **3.** B; **4.** A; **5.** C; **6.** A